What is Friendship?

Games and Activities to Help Children to Understand Friendship

Pamela Day

Jessica Kingsley Publishers
London and Philadelphia

of related interest

Asperger Syndrome in the Inclusive Classroom
Advice and Strategies for Teachers
Stacey W. Betts, Dion E. Betts and Lisa N. Gerber-Eckard
Foreword by Peter Riffle
ISBN: 978 1 84310 840 5

Fun with Messy Play
Ideas and Activities for Children with Special Needs
Tracey Beckerleg
ISBN: 978 1 84310 641 8

Helping Children with Complex Needs Bounce Back
Resilient Therapy™ for Parents and Professionals
Kim Aumann and Angie Hart
Illustrated by Chloe Gerhardt
ISBN: 978 1 84310 948 8

Helping Children to Build Self-Esteem
A Photocopiable Activities Book
2nd edition
Deborah M. Plummer
Illustrated by Alice Harper
ISBN: 978 1 84310 488 9

Challenge Me!™
Speech and Communication Cards
Amanda Elliott
Illustrated by David Kemp
ISBN: 978 1 84310 946 4

What Did You Say? What Do You Mean?
120 Illustrated Metaphor Cards, plus Booklet with Information, Ideas and Instructions
Jude Welton
Illustrated by Jane Telford
ISBN: 978 1 84310 924 2

Autism, Play and Social Interaction
Lone Gammeltoft and Marianne Sollok Nordenhof
Translated by Erik van Acker
ISBN: 978 1 84310 520 6

I would like to dedicate this book to my children,

Becki and Luke.

To thank them for all their help, advice and patience

whilst I practised new material on them

and for all the time compiling this

has taken me away from you.

I love you both very much.

Also, a very special thank you to Becki for the pictures.

First published in 2009
by Jessica Kingsley Publishers
116 Pentonville Road
London N1 9JB, UK
and
400 Market Street, Suite 400
Philadelphia, PA 19106, USA

www.jkp.com

Library of Congress Cataloging in Publication Data
A CIP catalog record for this book is available from the Library of Congress

British Library Cataloguing in Publication Data
A CIP catalogue record for this book is available from the British Library

ISBN 978 1 84905 048 7

Printed and bound in Great Britain by
Athenaeum Press, Gateshead, Tyne and Wear

Contents

Introduction

Children's mental health is being increasingly recognized as *everyone's business* and emotional health promotion is vital in terms of preventing mental health difficulties. There has been much research looking at the need for friendships, particularly in relation to children, and having a friend has been identified as a resilience factor in terms of preventing mental health difficulties.

We are social beings and having a sense of belonging is imperative to any child, and increases self esteem and feelings of self worth. Making friends and forming relationships are fundamental aspects of a child's social and emotional development.

However, developing relationships and friendships does not always occur naturally and can clearly be difficult for some children for a wide variety of reasons. As a very shy child, who did experience difficulties initiating relationships with my peers, I can identify how complex and daunting such a task can be.

This Activity Programme has been designed to assist children to develop their relationship skills. It has been designed in an easy to read, easy to use format with the intention of being used by any professional working with children aged 7–11 – whether in educational settings, health, social care or therapeutic settings (though note that the programme is not intended as a therapeutic intervention or substitute for therapy).

Although it is intended for children aged 7–11, the programme is flexible to any age group. The material has been used extensively in a range of settings, such as inclusive settings and with groups comprising children with a variety of diagnosed conditions such as ADHD (attention deficit hyperactivity disorder) and autism. Children with autism have been identified as having particular difficulties in relating to others and especially forming friendships.

It uses a variety of teaching techniques including role play and whole class activities as well as individual and small group work. The programme is designed to be run over six sessions of approximately 55 minutes duration, though it is also intended to be flexible. You can use the activities on a one-off basis, and deliver to an entire class or a select group of children – a smaller group can allow more opportunity for all children to contribute during circle time and the use of more appropriate plenaries.

The aims of the programme

The aims of the programme are for children:

- to be able to develop the knowledge and skills to initiate and maintain both new and established friendships

- to gain a greater understanding of their emotions and how this affects their friendships

- to be able to develop effective communication skills

- to develop the necessary knowledge, skills and confidence to resolve conflicts effectively

- to be aware of the effects of peer pressure within their relationships and how to deal with this effectively

- to work together as a group.

Identifying learning outcomes

The following knowledge, skills and understanding* are also taught within the programme:

- Preparing to play an active role as citizens: Resolving differences by looking at alternatives, making decisions and explaining choices.

- Developing a healthy, safer lifestyle: Pressure to behave in an unacceptable or risky way can come from a variety of sources, including people they know, and how to ask for help and use basic techniques for resisting pressure to do wrong.

- Developing good relationships and respecting the differences between people: Their actions affect themselves and others, to care about other people's feelings and to try to see things from their point of view. To be aware of different types of relationship,

including marriage and those between friends and families,
and to develop the skills to be effective in relationships.

(*In line with the PSHE (personal, social and health education) guidelines
for England and Wales, 2f, 3f, 4a, 4c.)

What have people said about the programme?

I would like to thank all the children, teachers and school nurses who have
participated in this programme and provided much appreciated feedback.
What children have said they have learnt from the programme:

About peer pressure where someone forces you
to do something and how to be a better friend.

Not to hit people.

How to stop bullying.

How to make friends.

Slugs are nasty words and bullying is wrong.

I wouldn't like it if someone bullied me so I
shouldn't bully anyone.

I learnt about how to treat people as my
friends.

I have made new friends.

I learnt how to listen to my friends.

I learnt that it is so easy just to say yes but I have
learnt to say no.

Teachers who didn't facilitate the programme:

>Taught the children useful strategies to help them deal with difficult situations.

>I have already noticed a change in the children's behaviour and their ability to relate to others.

Teachers and school nurses who facilitated the programme:

>The most useful element of the programme was the planning because it was clear and saved a lot of time.

>The individual lesson plans were excellent, easy to follow and saved a lot of time.

>The resources were great.

>The programme was easy to use and could be facilitated by anyone.

>The programme can be adapted to meet any age range.

Session 1: What is a Friend?

Activities

1.1 Introduction

1.2 Ground rules

1.3 What is a friend?

1.4 Who are our friends?

1.5 Conclusion and homework: How do we make friends?

Learning outcomes

At the end of this session, children will:

- know what 'being a friend' means
- be able to explain why friends are necessary
- be able to identify who their friends are
- know how to make new friends.

Resources required

Before you start this session, make sure you have the following:

- folder for each child (optional)
- flip chart
- pen
- Blu-Tack
- Post-it notes.

And the following handouts/worksheets:

- Friendship Ground Rules (p.56)
- Friendship Pie (p.57)
- Friends Agree/Disagree Game (p.58–61)
- My Friendship Circle (p.62)
- Making New Friends (p.63).

Activity 1.1: Introduction

TIME: 3 minutes

METHOD: Discussion

RESOURCES: Folder for every child

SAMPLE SCRIPT:

'Hello everyone, does anyone know who we are? My name is [xxxxx]' (introduce yourself and any other facilitators – who you are and what you do).

For example, if you are a school nurse, you can say:

'Does anyone know the difference between us and nurses who work in a hospital? Nurses in a hospital look after people who are poorly and I help to keep children like you well.

Does anyone know why we are here today? ...

We are going to be spending some time with you over the next six weeks/sessions and we're going to be talking about friendship.

Does anyone know what that means? ...

It is all about friends: what they are and why we need them. We will be doing lots of different things and you can keep all the work you do in the special folders on your desk.

These are especially for you; you don't have to show anyone if you don't want to. If, when you've finished all the sessions, you want to show someone like your parents or your friends, then you can do. You can decorate these folders if you want, and you can add your own work on friends, like if you want to make a drawing or write a story. It is entirely up to you.'

Activity 1.2: Ground rules

TIME: 12 minutes

METHOD: Discussion

RESOURCES: Friendship Ground Rules (p.56), a copy of the ground rules written on a flip chart, Friendship Pie (p.57), large sheet of paper with an empty pie drawn on

SAMPLE SCRIPT:

'The first thing we need to do, and you might think it is a bit boring but it is really important, is to set some ground rules. Have you ever done that before? …

[If not, explain they are a set of rules for us to stick to while we are in these sessions.]

Because we don't have a lot of time in these sessions we have already thought of some rules. [Distribute 'Friendship Ground Rules' and discuss each rule.]

Is there anything else anyone wants to add?…

[If so, add to flip chart – you can choose to use your own set of rules.]

We will all have a copy and we will put this on the wall to remind us all.

We are going to give you all a copy of "Friendship Pie".

[Distribute and go through each point.]

What we are hoping to do is make our own Friendship Pie. We are going to leave some little Post-it notes on your tables every week and if you think of some ingredients you would like to put in your Friendship Pie, you can write them on the notes.

So, if at any time you think of something, don't forget to write it down and then at the end of the session, you can add it. It is completely anonymous; you don't have to put your name on it so no-one will know what you want to put in the pie unless you tell them. Does everyone understand? I am going to make a start. I am going to put "honest" in the pie.'

Activity 1.3: What is a friend?

TIME: 25 minutes

METHOD: Whole group activity

RESOURCES: Friends Agree/Disagree Game (pp.58–61)

SAMPLE SCRIPT:

'We are going to play a little game now. You can see there are three signs on the wall which say "agree", "disagree" and "not sure".

I am going to read out a statement and I want you to decide if you agree, disagree or are unsure. If you agree, I want you to go and stand under the agree sign.

If you disagree, where do you go to stand? …

And if you aren't sure, where do you go? …

OK, are you ready?'

1. Read out a statement.

2. Discuss the reasons for the responses in each category *(agree, disagree, unsure)*.

3. If there is a lot of interaction you may not have time to read out each statement, in which case, choose the ones that you feel are more relevant to your group.

Activity 1.4: Who are our friends?

TIME: 10 minutes

METHOD: Individual work

RESOURCES: My Friendship Circle (p.62)

SAMPLE SCRIPT:

'So we know what friends are and why we need them. Shall we have a little think about who our friends are?

I am going to give you all a worksheet called "My Friendship Circle". [Distribute.]

What I want you to do is write your name in the centre of the circle and add all the people who are special to you; they can be friends, family or even pets.

Does everyone understand? …

I am not going to ask any of you to read them out, but I'd like you to keep them and we'll do that again at the end of our time with you and maybe you'll have some more names to add.'

Activity 1.5: Conclusion and homework: How do we make friends?

TIME: 5 minutes

METHOD: Discussion

RESOURCES: Making New Friends (p.63)

SAMPLE SCRIPT:

'We are just about finishing now, but has anyone any questions about anything from today? If anyone wants to say anything, I [and any other facilitators] will be around for a little while if you want to talk in private.

Before you go, I've got some work we'd like you to do for next week.

Each week we will be giving you a worksheet to do; maybe you'll have a chance to complete it during the session, but if not maybe you could do it at home. Now, it really is up to you whether you do it or not but you might find it will help you with the sessions we are going to be doing.

For next week, we'd like you to think about how you make friends. We have a worksheet to help you. It is about a couple of friends and a new girl in your school. How do you think they can become friends?'

Session 2: How do we choose our friends?

Activities

2.1: Introduction and review of homework

2.2: What do we look for in a friend?

2.3: Conclusion and homework: How do our friends help us? How do we help our friends?

Learning outcomes

At the end of this session, children will:

- identify qualities they look for in a friend

- identify their most important aspects of friendship

- understand the importance of help and co-operation to sustain friendships

- understand that opinions can differ.

Resources required

Before you start this session, make sure you have the following:

- flip chart
- pen
- Blu-Tack
- Post-it notes.

And the following handouts/worksheets:

- Friendship Ground Rules (p.56)
- Friendship Pie (p.57)
- Making New Friends (p.63)
- Qualities In A Friend (pp.64–72)
- To Have A Friend, You Need To Be A Friend (p.73)

Activity 2.1: Introduction and review of homework

TIME: 10 minutes

METHOD: Group discussion

RESOURCES: Friendship Ground Rules (p.56), Making New Friends (p.63), Post-it notes

SAMPLE SCRIPT:
'Hello again everyone. How are you? …

Can anyone remember what we talked about last week? …

[We talked about: what is a friend, who our friends are and how we make friends.]

Did anyone manage to complete the work from last week? …

Does anyone have any ideas how we can make friends with each other? …

[Brief discussion.]

Can I just remind you about the ground rules from last time; they will still apply today.

Don't forget if you have any ingredients for the Friendship Pie, add them at the end.'

Activity 2.2: What do we look for in a friend?

TIME: 35 minutes

METHOD: Whole group activity

RESOURCES: Qualities In A Friend (pp.64–72)

SAMPLE SCRIPT:

'What we are going to be talking about today is

How we choose our friends

and

What is it exactly about our friends that make them our friends?

[Place the "Important", "Very Important" and "Not Important" cards on the floor.]

You can see there are three cards: "Important", "Very Important" and "Not Important". You will all be given a card which has a quality or characteristic on it. You need to read the card and decide whether you think it is important, very important or not important that your friend has this.

If you think it is important, where do you put it? …

And if you think it is not important? …

After you have read your card out and placed it in the area that you think it should go, you will also get the chance to move one of the other cards if you don't agree with where it has been placed. Do you understand what you have to do?'

[After all the group have taken a turn, choose three children to act as 'captains' for each category. They then have to read out each characteristic/ quality under that category. Ask the group if they think this characteristic should stay in the category it is in or if it should go. This can then turn into a debate about where the characteristic should be placed. If opinion is divided, take a vote – ask another member of the group to count the vote, and apply a majority rule.]

Activity 2.3: Conclusion and homework: How do our friends help us? How do we help our friends?

TIME: 10 minutes

METHOD: Discussion

RESOURCES: To Have A Friend, You Need To Be A Friend (p.73)

SAMPLE SCRIPT:

'That shows how we all have different views: what is important to one person may not be important to another and that is because we are all individuals.

What I would like you to do for next week is think about how we can help our friends and how our friends can help us.

Has anyone ever heard of the saying "to have a friend, you need to be a friend"? …

Has anyone any idea what that means? …

That is the title of the worksheet for you to have a look at between now and next week.

Does anyone have any questions about anything today? …

Don't forget to put your ingredients in the Friendship Pie!'

Session 3: How do we communicate with our friends?

Activities

3.1 Introduction and review of homework

3.2 How do we talk to our friends?

3.3 How do we listen to our friends?

3.4 How do we use our bodies to show that we are listening?

3.5 Conclusion and homework: What can stop us listening?

Learning outcomes

At the end of this session, children will:

- be aware of the importance of effective communication
- be able to identify factors that help and hinder listening
- be able to initiate and maintain conversations with friends.

Resources required

Before you start this session, make sure you have the following:

- Blu-Tack

- Post-it notes.

And the following handouts/worksheets:

- Friendship Ground Rules (p.56)

- Friendship Pie (p.57)

- To Have A Friend, You Need To Be A Friend (p.73)

- Who (p.74)

- Script 1 (p.75)

- Script 2 (p.76)

- Are We Friends? (p.77)

- How Your Body Shows That You Are Listening (p.78)

- What Stops Me Listening? (p.79).

Activity 3.1: Introduction and review of homework

TIME: 5 minutes

METHOD: Discussion

RESOURCES: Friendship Ground Rules (p.56), Friendship Pie (p.57), homework from last week, To Have A Friend You Need To Be A Friend (p.73)

SAMPLE SCRIPT:

'Hello again everyone. How are you?

Can anyone remember what we talked about last week? (*We talked about what we look for in a friend.*)

What we are going to be talking about today is how we talk and listen to our friends.

But before that, did anyone manage to complete the work from last week?

So what sorts of things can we do to help our friends? How can our friends help us?

[Brief discussion.]

Can I just remind you all about the ground rules; they will still apply for today.

Don't forget if you have any ingredients for our Friendship Pie, add them at the end.

Today, we are talking about how we communicate with our friends.'

Activity 3.2: How do we talk to our friends?

TIME: 10 minutes

METHOD: Whole group activity

RESOURCES: Who (p.74)

SAMPLE SCRIPT:

'We're going to play a little game called Who...?

[Distribute 'Who' worksheet.]

What we want you to do is find someone who has done or likes something in one of the boxes. When you have matched a person to a box, write their initials in that box. You can use the same person for only one of the boxes.

[Allow about 8 minutes.]

How did you get on?

Has anyone managed to complete all their boxes?

How did you find out the information you needed?'

[By asking the right questions and listening to each other.]

Activity 3.3: How do we listen to our friends?

TIME: 20 minutes

METHOD: Role play, group discussion

RESOURCES: Script 1 (p.75), Script 2 (p.76), Are We Friends? (p.77), one co-facilitator to play at being a friend

SAMPLE SCRIPT:

'You've really got the hang of talking and listening to each other. We want your help now.

We are going to pretend to be friends at school; it is lunch time and we are in the playground. What we want you to do is watch and listen to what we say and do and then answer the questions on the sheet we are going to give you.

[Distribute 'Are We Friends?' worksheet. Act out Script 1.]

Are…and…friends? How do you know?

Was…listening to…? How do you know?

Were…and…talking to each other? How do you know?

Do you think anything could have been different? If so, what?

What about if we try that again and I take your advice this time?

[Act out Script 2.]

Do you think I was really listening to…this time?'

Activity 3.4: How do we use our bodies to show that we are listening?

TIME: 15 minutes

METHOD: Discussion, role play in pairs with feedback to group

RESOURCES: How Your Body Shows That You Are Listening (p.78)

SAMPLE SCRIPT:

'Do you think it is important to listen to each other? …

Now it's your turn. I want you to work in pairs with the person next to you and take it in turns to talk for 3 minutes but only about the subject I am going to give you.

Decide quickly who is going to be A and who is going to be B.

Have you decided? …

As: I want you to go first and talk about what you would do if you had a million pounds and you could spend it on anything you like.

[Time talk for 3 minutes.]

As: Do you think your partners were listening? …

Bs: Did you think you were listening? … Did you find yourselves thinking about what you'd do with a million pounds? …

We have a handout for you that gives you some advice about listening.

[Distribute 'How Your Body Shows That You Are Listening' and talk through each point.]

You are going to change around now and Bs are going to talk this time, about where you would go if you could go anywhere in the world and why.

This time, As, think about what your body is doing and practise something from the handout.

[Time talk for 3 minutes.]

Bs: Do you think your partners were listening? ... Did you notice anybody using any of the skills on the handout? ... If so, which? ...

As: Did you think you were listening? ... Did you find yourselves thinking about where you'd go? ... Did you use any of the skills? ... If so, which? ...

Are you going to try and remember to really listen? ...'

Activity 3.5: Conclusion and homework: What can stop us listening?

TIME: 5 minutes

METHOD: Discussion

RESOURCES: What Stops Me Listening? (p.79)

SAMPLE SCRIPT:

'For next week, we want you to think about what sorts of things can stop you from listening.

Sometimes, we can hear what is being said but we don't always listen, like when I was talking to…, I wasn't really listening to her, was I?

Has anyone got any questions from anything today? Once again,…and I will stay behind if anyone wants to see us in private.

Don't forget to put your ingredients in the Friendship Pie!'

Session 4: How do we resolve conflict?

Activities

4.1 Introduction and review of homework

4.2 Why do we have conflict?

4.3 What can we do about conflict?

4.4 How do we deal with conflict?

4.5 Conclusion: Conflict questionnaire

Learning outcomes

At the end of this session, children will:

- know what is meant by conflict

- be able to identify how and why conflict arises

- be able to resolve conflict effectively.

Resources required

Before you start this session, make sure you have the following:

- Post-it notes
- Blu-Tack
- lidded box to keep 'slugs' in.

And the following handouts/worksheets:

- Friendship Ground Rules (p.56)
- Friendship Pie (p.57)
- What Stops Me Listening? (p.79)
- Slugs Script (pp.80–81)
- Slugs Cards (pp.82–84)
- Extension To 'Slugs' Activity (pp85–86)
- Ways To Solve An Argument (p.87)
- Conflict Scenarios (pp.88–89)
- Conflict Questionnaire (p.90).

Activity 4.1: Introduction and review of homework

TIME: 5 minutes

METHOD: Discussion

RESOURCES: Friendship Ground Rules (p.56), Friendship Pie (p.57) *(both to be put on wall prior to session)*, homework from last week, What Stops Me Listening (p.79)

SAMPLE SCRIPT:
'Hello again everyone. How are you? …

Can anyone remember what we talked about last week? …

[We talked about listening and talking to friends.]

Did anyone manage to think of anything that stops you listening? …

Can I just remind you all about the ground rules; they will still apply for today. Don't forget if you have any ingredients for our Friendship Pie, add them at the end.

What we are going to be talking about today is conflict. Does anyone know what a conflict is? …

It means having an argument or disagreement with someone.

Put your hand up if you have ever had a conflict with someone.'

Activity 4.2: Why do we have conflict?

TIME: 20 minutes

METHOD: Role play, group discussion, pair work

RESOURCES: Slugs Script (pp.80–81), Slugs Cards (pp.82–84), lidded box to keep 'slugs' in (alternatively, the activity may be adapted to use other insects or words, such as 'worms', to describe name calling, or the Extension To 'Slugs' Activity (pp.85–86) can be used to elaborate further upon name calling)

SAMPLE SCRIPT:

[Go straight into acting out 'Slugs' without any further explanation – see pp. 80–81.]

'We see slugs all the time, don't we? We even throw them around at times. Sometimes we even forget why we are doing it.

How does it feel to throw a slug?

How does it feel if you are the one the slug is being thrown at?

What can we do about it? We don't have to catch it for a start.

How about if we stop to think before we throw a slug?

If a slug is being thrown at us, we don't have to catch it. We could ignore what the person throwing the slug has said, couldn't we?

When we are feeling a bit angry or upset or even just plain mean, when we say something not nice to someone, let's imagine it really is a slug and stop and think how we would feel if the slug was being thrown at us.

Work in pairs for a few minutes with the person sitting next to you; take it in turns to say something nice to each other.

[Allow 3 minutes.]

Did you do that? …

Was it easy or difficult to say something nice? …

Was it easy or difficult to hear something nice being said about you? …'

Activity 4.3: What can we do about conflict?

TIME: 10 minutes

METHOD: Group discussion

RESOURCES: Ways To Solve An Argument (p.87)

SAMPLE SCRIPT:

'It is highly unlikely that any of you will go through life without any sort of conflict.

Everybody falls out with someone for some reason or another.

Part of being friends is being able to have the confidence to disagree and to say how you are feeling, but what about when it gets to be more than that?

We have a handout to give you with ways you can solve an argument, some of which you have already mentioned.'

[Distribute 'Ways To Solve An Argument' handout and read through.]

Activity 4.4: How do we deal with conflict?

TIME: 15 minutes

METHOD: Buzz groups

RESOURCES: Conflict Scenarios (pp.88–89)

SAMPLE SCRIPT:

'Now, it is time for you to have a practice.

We are going to give each table a card with a different situation on, describing a conflict. What we would like you to do is work together as a group on deciding how you would deal with that conflict.

[Distribute 'Conflict Scenarios'.]

[Time – 5 minutes.]

How did you get on?

Did you have any ideas how you could help to resolve the conflict?

Did everyone in your group agree or was there conflict within the group deciding on what to do?'

Activity 4.5: Conclusion: Conflict questionnaire

TIME: 5 minutes

METHOD: Discussion

RESOURCES: Conflict Questionnaire (p.90)

SAMPLE SCRIPT:

'We have a conflict questionnaire for you to do for next time.

[Distribute worksheet.]

Does anyone have any questions from anything we have talked about today?

Once again, if anyone wants to talk to…or me in private, we will stay behind for a few minutes.

Don't forget to put your ingredients in the Friendship Pie.'

Session 5: How do we deal with peer pressure?

Activities

5.1 Introduction and review of homework: What is peer pressure?

5.2 Who makes our decisions?

5.3 Positive and negative peer pressure

5.4 How do we deal with negative peer pressure?

5.5 Conclusion

Learning outcomes

At the end of this session, children will:

- understand what is meant by positive and negative peer pressure

- identify a range of strategies to deal with negative peer pressure

- understand the concept of decision making.

Resources required

Before you start this session, make sure you have:

- flip chart
- pen
- Post-it notes
- Blu-tack
- boxes of sweets/candy cigarettes.

And the following handouts/worksheets:
- Friendship Ground Rules (p.56)
- Friendship Pie (p.57)
- Conflict Questionnaire (p.90)
- Peer Pressure Sketch (p.91)
- Who Makes My Decisions? (p.92)
- Five Ways To Deal With Negative Peer Pressure (p.93).
- Peer Pressure Sketch 2 (p.94)

Activity 5.1: Introduction and review of homework: What is peer pressure?

TIME: 12 minutes

METHOD: Role play, group discussion

RESOURCES: Friendship Ground Rules (p.56), Friendship Pie (p.57), homework from last session, Conflict Questionnaire (p.90), Peer Pressure Sketch (p.91)

SAMPLE SCRIPT:
[Start immediately with the Peer Pressure Sketch, p.91.]

'That was to show you what sort of things we say to our friends to try to get them to do what we want them to.

Was any of it familiar? …

Has anyone ever said or heard any of the things we were saying? …

What we are talking about today is peer pressure. Has anyone any idea what that means? …

It means how we are influenced by our friends.

But first, did anyone manage to complete their conflict questionnaires? Has anyone anything they'd like to say about it? …

Can I just remind you all about the ground rules; they will still apply today.

Don't forget if you have any ingredients for our Friendship Pie, add them at the end.'

Activity 5.2: Who makes our decisions?

TIME: 13 minutes

METHOD: Group discussion, individual work

RESOURCES: Who Makes My Decisions? (p.92)

SAMPLE SCRIPT:

'Let's talk about decisions. Who do you think makes our decisions? …

We are going to have a little quiz which looks at who makes our decisions.

[Distribute 'Who Makes My Descisions?' worksheet.]

We want you to work through the quiz quickly; don't spend too long thinking about each question.

[Allow 5 minutes.]

Were there any surprises from that? …

Who makes the most decisions? …

Why do you think that is? …

Is there a big difference between the decisions you make and the decisions your parents make? …'

Activity 5.3: Positive and negative peer pressure

TIME: 5 minutes

METHOD: Discussion

RESOURCES: N/A

SAMPLE SCRIPT:

'We have looked at decision making and we have an idea what peer pressure is but did you know that there are two types of peer pressure: positive and negative?

If a friend was encouraging you to revise for a test rather then watching TV, which sort of peer pressure would that be? ...

[Positive.]

What about if your friend was encouraging you to watch TV rather than revising for a test? ...

[That would be negative.]

Which is easier to deal with, the positive or the negative? ...'

Activity 5.4: How do we deal with negative peer pressure?

TIME: 15 minutes

METHOD: Pair work, role play, group discussion

RESOURCES: Boxes of sweets/candy cigarettes, Five Ways To Deal With Negative Peer Pressure (p.93), Peer Pressure Sketch 2 (p.94), two facilitators to run the activity

SAMPLE SCRIPT:

'Now, it is your turn to practise dealing with negative peer pressure.

We want you to find a partner quickly and decide who is going to be "A" and who is going to be "B".

As, I want you to go with…who will give you some instructions.

[Take As outside and tell them their job is to say no to whatever Bs ask them to do.]

Give Bs a box of sweets/candy cigarettes. Explain to Bs that their job will be to try to convince their partners to take the cigarette. Tell them to try a variety of ways to get them to take the cigarette.

Bring As back into the room.

[Allow 3 minutes.]

As:

Did any of you take the cigarette/sweet? If so, what prompted you to take it?

What were you thinking when your partner was trying to convince you to take the sweet?

What were you feeling?

Bs:

What were you thinking when you were trying to convince your partner to take the sweet?

What were you feeling? If your partner took the sweet, how did you feel?

Have you ever been in a situation when someone tried to convince you to do something you didn't want to or you knew you shouldn't do?

Has anyone any ideas what you can do to resist negative peer pressure?

We have a handout that tells you about five ways to deal with negative peer pressure.

[Distribute 'Five Ways To Deal With Negative Peer Pressure' handout and go through each point.]

We are going to act out a scene using these methods. See if you can identify any of them.'

[Act out 'Peer Pressure Sketch 2'. Re-iterate each point.]

Activity 5.5: Conclusion: Preparing to say goodbye

TIME: 10 minutes

METHOD: Discussion

RESOURCES: N/A

SAMPLE SCRIPT:

'You will be pleased to know you do not have any homework this week.

What we would like you to do now though is to decide if there is anything you would like to do next week.

We have our Friendship Pie to make, but we have left a little time free for you to decide what to do.

Is there anything we have done over the last five weeks that you would like to see or do again? It is up to you. Have a little think about it for a few minutes and then we will have a vote.

Have you decided?

[Use majority vote if lots of views.]

Do not forget to put your ingredients in the Friendship Pie.'

Session 6: What have we learnt?

Activities

6.1 Introduction
6.2 Who are our friends?
6.3 As decided by the group
6.4 Friendship pie
6.5 Conclusion and goodbyes

Learning outcomes

At the end of this session, children will:

- evaluate what they have learnt.

Resources required

Before you start this session, make sure you have:

- flip chart
- pen
- Post-it notes
- Blu-tack

And the following handouts/worksheets:

- Friendship Ground Rules (p.56)
- Friendship Pie (p.57)
- My Friendship Circle (p.62)
- What Did You Think? (p.95)
- Certificate (p.96)

Activity 6.1: Introduction

TIME: 5 minutes

METHOD: Group discussion

RESOURCES: Friendship Ground Rules (p.56), Friendship Pie (p.57) *(both to be put on wall prior to session)*

SAMPLE SCRIPT:

'Hello everyone and welcome to the last of our friendship sessions. We hope you have all enjoyed them as much as we have.

What do we have to remember as always? The ground rules.'

Activity 6.2: Who are our friends?

TIME: 5 minutes

METHOD: Individual work

RESOURCES: My Friendship Circle (p.62)

SAMPLE SCRIPT:

'Before we do [the activity of the children's choice], do you remember when we first started, we did My Friendship Circle to see who our friends are? I would like us to do that again, just to see if anything has changed.

[Distribute 'My Firendship Circle' worksheet and allow a few minutes for completion.]

I do not want to see any of them but does anyone want to mention anything?

Has anyone added any new names?'

Activity 6.3: As decided by the group

TIME: 15 minutes

METHOD: As original activity

RESOURCES: As original activity

SAMPLE SCRIPT: As original activity

Activity 6.4: Friendship pie

TIME: 15 minutes

METHOD: Group discussion

RESOURCE: Friendship Pie (p.57)

SAMPLE SCRIPT:

'Right, let us look at our Friendship Pie. It looks like it is going to be a fantastic pie, full of lots of lovely things.'

[Talk through each ingredient in the pie.]

Activity 6.5: Conclusion and goodbyes

TIME: 15 minutes

METHOD: Pair work

RESOURCES: What Did You Think? (p.95), Certificate (p.96)

SAMPLE SCRIPT:

'We have come to the end of our time together now and both...and I would like to say a very big thank you to you all for all the hard work you have done.

I would like you to work with a partner and spend a few minutes talking about what you have learnt from the What is Friendship? Programme.

[Allow a few minutes and ask if anyone would like to share with the group.]

We really hope you keep up the good work and remember what you have learnt.

Now before we go, we would like you to complete a feedback form because it is important to us what you have thought about the programme.

We need you to be honest and if you think we need to change some parts of the programme please say so. You do not need to put your name on the form.

[Distribute 'What Did You Think?' form.]

Now, we would like to give you all your certificates.'

[Give each child a certificate.]

Appendix: Extension ideas

Once you have familiarized yourself with the chapters, spend some time thinking about additional activities you could do with the children – below are some suggestions to get your creativity flowing!

- Make a collage or other art work depicting friendship.
- Identify famous friends.
- Write a story or poem about friendship.
- Read stories about friendship.
- Ask everyone to talk about a friend or someone special to them, explaining why this person is special.
- Make up a 'perfect' friend.
- Build a friendship scrapbook.
- Interview other people such as relatives asking who their friends are, were, if these have changed over the years, etc.
- Friendship songs.
- Word search puzzle.
- Make and act out a play.
- Diamond nine game looking at the qualities we look for in a friend.
- Select a collection of photographs of people talking and ask the children if they think these people may be friends to stimulate conversation regarding friendship.

- Think about plenaries that can be devised following the programme. For example:

  o Each member of the group (children and adults) could be given a card with a picture of a thumb on. In turn, they display the thumb that shows how they feel the session went and what they had learnt and took away from the session: thumbs up for a good session, thumbs down for a bad session, or in the middle for unsure. They also explain the reason for their choice of positioning.

  o The children could perform some of the sketches before a whole school assembly – perhaps the slugs and peer pressure sketches – and talk about the programme and what it involved.

Handouts

✓

Friendship
Ground Rules

Listen when others are speaking

There is no such thing as a silly question!

Put your hand up if you want to speak

Only one person can talk at a time

You don't have to say anything if you don't want

Do not laugh at each other

It is OK to tell other people what you have learnt in the classroom but it is *not* OK to share anything secret or confidential with people who are not in the classroom.

Friendship Pie

- Make the base with fun and games

- Add two teaspoons of trust

- Stir a warm smile into the mixture

- Mix a cup of outings

- Add a pinch of conversation

- Don't forget a shoulder to cry on as a special treat

- Put the pie in the oven for an hour at 200 degrees

- Take it out and let it cool for a few minutes, patience is a safety ingredient

- Cut it into enough pieces for you and your friends to share

Friends Agree/Disagree Game

1. We need friends

2. Friends are important

3. You stop having friends when you grow up

4. Everyone has friends

5. It is easy to make friends

6. If you don't have friends it means there is something wrong with you

7. You have to have lots of friends and not just one

8. If you have an argument with your friend, it means you will never be friends again

9. Your parents can be your friends

10. Boys can only have friends who are boys and girls can only have friends who are girls

11. You have to be grown up to have a boyfriend or a girlfriend

12. If your friend is in trouble, you should help even if it means you would get in trouble too

✓

Agree

✓

Disagree

Not Sure

My Friendship Circle

Write your name in the centre of the circle.
Think about people you know in your life, and place them
in the circles surrounding you, according to how close
(important) you feel they are to you

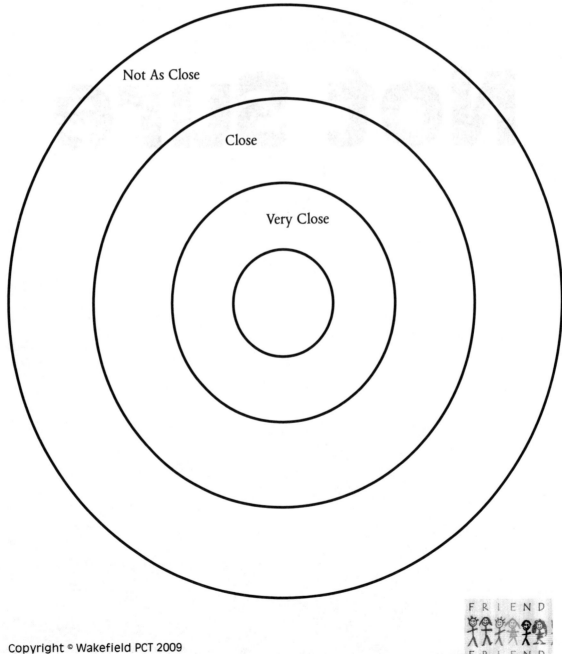

Making New Friends

Laura has just moved to a new school. She has left a lot of her friends behind and is feeling very lonely. She wants to make some new friends but is very shy and doesn't know what to do!

**What do you think Laura can say or
do to make friends?**

Megan and Kathryn have been friends for a long time. They have seen the new girl but don't know her name. They would like to be her friend but don't know what to say or do!

What do you think Megan and Kathryn can say or do to make Laura their friend?

63

✓

Qualities In A Friend

To be cut out and laminated:

Sticks Up For Me	Good At Sport
Likes The Same Things As Me	Is Interesting
Likes Music	Cares For Other People

Is Always Happy	Wears Nice Clothes
Is Helpful	Is Clever
Is Honest	Listens To Me

✓

Is Kind	Is Respectful
Is Polite	Supports Me
Is The Same Sex As Me	Is The Same Age As Me

Likes To Have Fun	Is Good Looking
Is Popular	Is Funny
Has Lots Of Money	Is Liked By My Parents

✓

Has All The Latest Games	Doesn't Go Off With Other People
Will Keep My Secrets	Doesn't Bully Other People
Understands Me	Knows What I Like

✓

Buys Me Things	Tells the Truth (Even If It Hurts My Feelings)
Will Do Anything For Me (Even If It Means Getting Into Trouble)	Doesn't Mind If I Want To Be Alone
Shares	Will Do Everything I Say

✓

Important

Very Important

✓

Not Important

To Have A Friend,
You Need To Be A Friend

What does this statement mean?

Do you agree or disagree with it?

How do good friends treat each other?

What sort of things does your friend do to help you?

What sort of things do you do to help your friend?

Who

Find someone who matches the description in each of the boxes.
Write their initials in the matching box.
You can only use the same person once.

Likes Singing	Plays Cricket	Rides A Bike	Can Dance
Has A Blue Car	Plays Football	Has Been In A Plane	Can Skateboard
Owns A Dog	Has A Caravan	Has A PlayStation	Likes Pizza
Has Been Skiing	Plays An Instrument	Likes Rollercoaster Rides	Grows Vegetables

Script 1

PERSON 1 Hi. What's the matter? Are you coming to play?

PERSON 2 Sally is being mean to me; she says I am smelly and stupid.

PERSON 1 Oh, is that it? I thought someone had died or something!

PERSON 2 But she keeps calling me names!

PERSON 1 Don't be a cry baby, come and play. Sally knows a new game.

PERSON 2 But...

PERSON 1 *(interrupting)* What is the matter with you? Come on or she'll show it to the others.

PERSON 2 But she says...

PERSON 1 *(interrupting)* Oh, you are so boring; I am off to play with Sally.

✓

Script 2

PERSON 1 Hi. What's the matter?

PERSON 2 *Sally is being mean to me!*

PERSON 1 What is she doing?

PERSON 2 *She keeps calling me names; she says I am smelly and stupid!*

PERSON 1 That is not a nice thing to say. Shall we go and tell Miss?

PERSON 2 *OK.*

Are We Friends?

Watch and listen to ……………………………..
and ………………………… talking to each other
and answer the following questions.

Enter the names of the people doing the sketch on the dotted lines.

1. Are ……………… and ……………friends?

Yes ☐   No ☐   Unsure ☐

2. How do you know?

3. Was …………… listening to ………………..?

Yes ☐   No ☐   Unsure ☐

4. How do you know?

5. Were ………….. and …………… talking to each other?

Yes ☐   No ☐   Unsure ☐

6. How do you know?

7. Do you think anything could have been different?

Yes ☐   No ☐   Unsure ☐

8. If so, what?

✓

How Your Body Shows That You Are Listening

BRAIN

Thinks… 'What Is The Person Saying?'
'Do I Understand This?'
'Do I Look Like I Am Really Listening?'

HEAD

NODS OCCASIONALLY

EYES

Looks At The Person
Stays Open

MOUTH

IS QUIET WHEN SOMEONE IS TALKING
DOES NOT YAWN, DOES NOT INTERRUPT

BODY

Faces The Person They Are Talking To
Does Not Move Around Too Much
Uses Appropriate Posture

What Stops Me Listening?

Add all the things you can think of that stop
you listening properly inside the stars.

These can be things inside your body like being hungry
or things outside your body like loud music.

Two have already been completed for you!

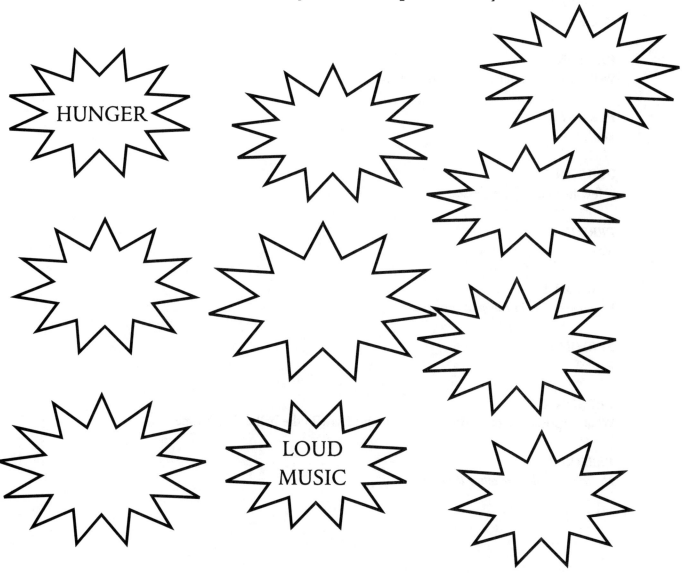

Slugs Script

PERSON 1

You know ...., we have been in this school a few weeks now.
While we have been here, I have been walking around and I have found a lot of slugs.

PERSON 2

Slugs?

PERSON 1

Yep, slugs!

PERSON 2

Where did you find them?

PERSON 1

Well, there were quite a lot in the playground.

PERSON 2

Really?

PERSON 1

A few in some of the classes.

PERSON 2

No?

PERSON 1

I even saw one in the staff room.

PERSON 2

Really?

PERSON 1

What surprised me the most was the amount I saw in the hall at lunch time.

PERSON 2

No, while people were eating their dinner?

PERSON 1

Yes, some people were even throwing them around the tables.

PERSON 2

Oh, that's not nice, is it?

PERSON 1

Whenever I have seen a slug, I have kept it and put it in this box. There's a massive collection now.

PERSON 2

The box does feel quite full. Do you think we should show the children?

PERSON 1

I don't know, shall we ask them? Would you like to see some slugs?

Take the lid off the bucket and pretend to throw the slugs at the children (but throw them on the floor, in front of you).

PERSON 1

Pick up and read some of the slugs out.

PERSON 2

These are the nasty things we sometimes say to each other. If we think of them as slugs, imagine how hurtful it is when someone throws one at us.

PERSON 1

We wouldn't like someone to throw a slug at us, would we?

PERSON 2

So, it isn't nice to throw one either, is it?

PERSON 1

Let's all remember next time we say one of those horrible things like 'you're gay' or 'no one likes you'.

PERSON 2

That it really is a slug and think before we throw it.

Thank You!

Adapted from 'Don't Shoot!' We may both be on the same side. A curriculum guide for working together and resolving conflicts. Kathy Beckwith. 1988, Minneapolis, Education Media Corporation.

Slugs Cards

To be cut out and laminated:

No One Wants To Go Out With You

You're Gay

No One Likes You

Go Away

Don't Play With Him

He's Like A Girl

✓

Weirdo	Show Off
Stupid	Freak
Cry Baby	Ugly

Extension To 'Slugs' Activity

After you have 'thrown the slugs':

PERSON 1
How do you think it feels to have a slug thrown at you? *(Ask the children)*
Shall we find out? Shall I throw a slug at *(Person 2…substitute name)* and see how it makes her/him feel?

PERSON 1
Throw a slug (such as I don't like you).

PERSON 2
Looks hurt and upset.

PERSON 1
How do you think *(Person 2)* feels? Would someone like to ask her?

Ask for one of the children to come to the front and ask how (Person 2) feels.

PERSON 1
What do you think *(Person 2)* could have done instead of catching the slug?

Use an option that the children have shouted out, such as walk away.

PERSON 1
Shall we see how *(Person 2)* feels if she walks away?

Again, throw a slug and Person 2 walks away (Person 1 could follow and repeat slug throwing).

Ask for one of the children to come to the front and ask Person 2 how it felt to not catch the slug but walk away.

Try another option shouted out by the children, such as tell an adult or teacher.

Ask one of the children to come to the front to be a teacher.
Person 1 again throws a slug at Person 2 who then goes and tells the 'teacher' (talk about what your school would do if someone was bullying).

Congratulate the 'teacher' and ask them to return to their seat; ask someone else to the front to ask Person 2 how it felt telling someone.

Discuss how difficult it can be to tell someone but how this can be a really good thing and what could help, such as talking to someone else, taking a friend, etc.

Use another option, such as throw a slug back. This time Person 1 and Person 2 throw slugs at each other.

Ask the children what would have happened if the teacher had walked in (both got into trouble, etc.).

PERSON 1
So we talked about how it feels to throw slugs and how it feels to have a slug thrown at you. What about if your friends are making you throw slugs at each other? Sometimes people may throw slugs because other people do it and they think if they don't, they won't be friends any more. *(Open discussion.)*

PERSON 1
Do you think I have been mean to (*Person 2*)? What do you think I should do now? Say sorry?

Pretend to say sorry in a variety of incorrect ways, such as shouting, not looking at (Person 2), saying it quietly, saying it dramatically and sarcastically, saying it and then throwing a slug.

Ask for help from the children to say sorry properly.

End the session by reiterating the points discussed and congratulating the children for their input.

Ways to Solve An Arguement

✓

Take Turns

Agree On A Totally Different Idea

Combine Your Ideas

Find A Friend Who Can Talk With You Both

Draw Straws Or Toss A Coin

Agree To Disagree

✓

Conflict Scenarios

You are playing netball with your friends. Emma and Kelly grabbed the ball at the same time and neither of them would let it go. **What do you do?**	Your little brother is calling you names. You shout at him but he cries and goes to tell your mum. Your mum is cross with you and tells you to be nice. **What do you do?**
It is your auntie's party. You want to wear your new trousers but your mum wants you to wear something really horrible. **What do you do?**	You were waiting patiently in line and Danny pushed in front of you. **What do you do?**
Your parents have said you and your brother can decide where to go on holiday next year. You want to go to Disney World but your brother wants to go to Spain. You don't think it is fair that he should get his own way just because he is younger than you! **What do you do?**	You are playing on the computer with your friend. You want to play a football game but he wants to play an army game. You always have to play what he wants because he says it is his computer! **What do you do?**

It is playtime at school and you all want to play a different game. **What do you do?**	Charlie loves cricket and Billy loves football. They are arguing about which is best. **What do you do?**
You borrowed your sister's mobile phone but your friend has just dropped it on the floor. **What do you do?**	You have just tidied your bedroom and your little brother comes in and throws paper all over the floor. Your mum shouts, 'Get your bedroom tidy – it is a tip!' **What do you do?**
You are going on an outing in the car with your family. Your brother always sits near the window but you want a turn and he won't let you. **What do you do?**	You see two of your friends fighting in the playground. **What do you do?**

✓

Conflict Questionnaire

1. Can you describe a conflict (argument) you had recently?
2. Who was the conflict with?
3. Why did it happen?
4. How did you feel?
5. How do you think the other person felt?
6. What did you do about it?
7. Did it resolve the conflict? (Make it better?)
8. Do you think you could have done anything differently?

Peer Pressure Sketch

✓

NB: MAKE SURE THE CHILDREN ARE ALL SEATED IN THE ROOM READY BEFORE YOU START THIS SKETCH

PERSON 1 AND PERSON 2 WALKING INTO ROOM

PERSON 1:
Oh come on, please ……………….. I'll give you a Mars Bar if you do…

PERSON 2:
No!

PERSON 1:
Why not? You've done it before ………… Oh go on, it will be really good. Come on, everyone does it ………………… What's the matter, are you stupid or what?

PERSON 2:
DOES NOT SPEAK, SHAKES HEAD

PERSON 1:
Oh go on, it will be really good. You have to because I helped you last week ……….. Why not, you've done it before ……………… I won't talk to you any more. I won't be your friend!

PERSON 2:
DOES NOT SPEAK

PERSON 1:
Well, fair enough, do the class on your own then!
ANGRILY STORMS OUT OF ROOM

✓

Who Makes My Decisions?

Who decides?

1. What TV programme I watch?				
MYSELF ☐	PARENTS ☐	TEACHERS ☐	FRIENDS ☐	UNSURE ☐
2. What I wear?				
MYSELF ☐	PARENTS ☐	TEACHERS ☐	FRIENDS ☐	UNSURE ☐
3. What I eat?				
MYSELF ☐	PARENTS ☐	TEACHERS ☐	FRIENDS ☐	UNSURE ☐
4. What I learn at school?				
MYSELF ☐	PARENTS ☐	TEACHERS ☐	FRIENDS ☐	UNSURE ☐
5. What time I go to bed?				
MYSELF ☐	PARENTS ☐	TEACHERS ☐	FRIENDS ☐	UNSURE ☐
6. What music I listen to?				
MYSELF ☐	PARENTS ☐	TEACHERS ☐	FRIENDS ☐	UNSURE ☐
7. What football team I support (if any)?				
MYSELF ☐	PARENTS ☐	TEACHERS ☐	FRIENDS ☐	UNSURE ☐
8. How much homework I get?				
MYSELF ☐	PARENTS ☐	TEACHERS ☐	FRIENDS ☐	UNSURE ☐
9. What I do on a weekend?				
MYSELF ☐	PARENTS ☐	TEACHERS ☐	FRIENDS ☐	UNSURE ☐
10. How much money I have to spend?				
MYSELF ☐	PARENTS ☐	TEACHERS ☐	FRIENDS ☐	UNSURE ☐

Five Ways To Deal With Negative Peer Pressure

Say no…
and continue to say no

Sense of humour…
just make a joke of it

Ignore…just walk away

Tell someone

Give a reason why
you don't want to

Peer Pressure Sketch 2

PERSON 1: Would you like a cigarette?

PERSON 2: No.

PERSON 1: Why not?

PERSON 2: No thanks, I don't smoke. I think they are bad for you.

PERSON 1: Come on, everyone does it.

PERSON 2: **SHAKES HEAD AND SAYS NO**

PERSON 1: What's the matter, are you stupid or what?

PERSON 2: You must be joking; I'm not the stupid one for wanting to smoke!
(SAY THIS WHILST LAUGHING)

PERSON 1: Go on, you know you want one. I won't talk to you any more. I won't be your friend.

PERSON 2: **SHAKES HEAD AND STARTS TO WALK AWAY**

PERSON 1: I will tell everyone that you are a big baby.

PERSON 2: I am off now to tell Miss.

PERSON 1: In that case, I am off too!

What Did You Think?

✓

1. How much did you like the lessons? Brilliant ☐   Good ☐   Not Much ☐   Boring ☐
2. How much did you learn? Lots ☐   Quite A Bit ☐   Not Much ☐   Nothing ☐
3. What did you like the most?
4. What didn't you like?
5. Are there any changes you would like to make to the programme?
6. Is there anything else you would like to add to the programme?

✓

FRIEND
FRIEND

Certificate

WELL DONE

To

For completion of

THE FRIENDSHIP PROGRAMME

What is a friend?
Who are our friends?
How do we make friends?
What do we look for in a friend?
How do our friends help us?
How do we help our friends?
How do we talk to our friends?
How do we listen to our friends?
How do we use our bodies to show
that we are listening?
What can stop us listening?
What is a conflict?
Why do we have conflict?
What can we do about conflict?
How do we deal with conflict?
What is peer pressure?
Who makes our decisions?
Positive and negative peer pressure
How do we deal with negative peer pressure?
Who are our friends?
Friendship pie

Signed: Date: